W9-BJO-114

Purr Purr Purr

Purr Purr Purr

Purr Purr Purr

Purr Purr P

Purr

Scratch Sc

Purr Purr P

Purr Purr Pu

Purr Purr

Purr Purr P

Purr Purr

Purr Purr
Purr

Purr Purr

Purr

lick · lick lick

ty lickety lick

lick lick lick

lick lick li

cough cough co

h ← furball la

lick · lick li

ty lick lick l

ick lick lick lick

ty lickety licke

ITTY
BITTY
KITTY
DITTIES

Artist
Alex Boies

designer
Jo Davison

Writer
Tim Hodapp

Abrams Image, New York

For more information and for other Itty Bitty Kitty goods, visit
www.kittyditties.com.

Editor: David Cashion
Designer: Jo Davison
Production Manager: Jacqueline Poirier

Library of Congress Cataloging-in-Publication Data

Boies, Alex.
  Itty bitty kitty ditties / illustrated by Alex Boies ; text by Tim
Hodapp ; designed by Jo Davison.
      p. cm.
  Includes bibliographical references and index.
  ISBN 978-0-8109-9639-7 (alk. paper)
  1. Cats—Caricatures and cartoons. 2. Cats—Poetry. I. Hodapp,
Tim. II. Title.

  NC1429.B658A4 2009
  741.5'6973—dc22
                                            2008030408

Printed and bound in China
10 9 8 7 6 5 4 3 2 1

Abrams Image books are available at special discounts when
purchased in quantity for premiums and promotions as well as
fundraising or educational use. Special editions can also be created to
specification. For details, contact specialmarkets@hnabooks.com or
the address below.

HNA
harry n. abrams, inc.
a subsidiary of La Martinière Groupe
115 West 18th Street
New York, NY 10011
www.hnabooks.com

This little book is inspired by
and dedicated to Tim Gray,
Big Foot, and of course Puddy,
with love for all!

Alex Boies

Agnes the cat
ambled all day by herself,
and then, quite content,
settled down on a shelf.

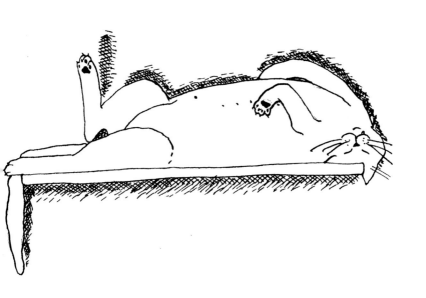

Agnes

Baxter the cat
bit a large bird on its beak
and refused to release it
for more than a week.

Baxter

C

Carmen the cat
cased the basement each night,
with her eyes on the corner
and her paw on the light.

Carmen

Dylan the cat
designed a dog-hair collection.
He snipped while they scratched,
thus evading detection.

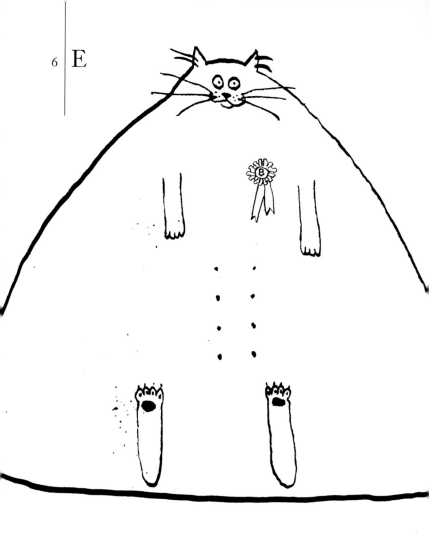

Edith the cat
earned eighth place at the show
with her full feline figure
and face all aglow.

Franklin

Franklin the cat
felt an urge for a treat.
Why settle for canned
when there's fresh fish to eat?

Greta

Greta the cat
got glue gobs on her paws.
Though she cleaned up good,
she still lost her claws.

Hubert

o ~meow

oh
Solo
Meow

Hubert the cat
harbored a hatred for hounds
and haunted them daily
with unholy sounds.

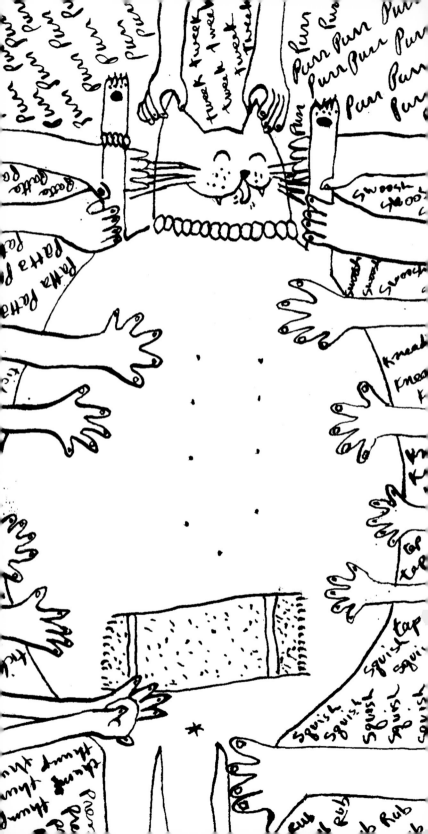

Ivy the cat
(irate with an itch)
had ten groomers come groom her
(her mistress was rich)!

Julian

Julian the cat
jumped into the john
with a bad case of the runs
that his fish oil brought on.

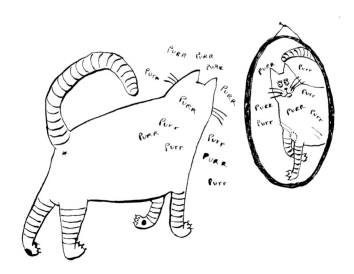

Katie the cat
kissed herself in the mirror,
and then purred, "Farewell,"
without shedding a tear.

Lionel the cat
lied when the truth fit him better.
"Then, pray tell, who
took a nap on my sweater?"

Madeline the cat
manicured her nails with finesse,
yet she tore through the sofa
when under duress.

Madeline

Neville

Neville the cat
never napped in the nude.
He even wore jammies
when not in the mood.

O

Opal the cat
often coughed up a few hairs,
then she'd resume her grooming,
ignoring the stares.

Basic Fur Balls

Puddy

Puddy the cat,
pitch black, barely stirred,
batting two large, green eyes
from a shadow that purred.

Queenie

Queenie the cat,
quite quick with a quill,
found postage for letters
depleted her till.

Hair Erectus

Not Safe

Rupert the cat
rang a brass bell for his mice
and enjoyed them with toast points
and vodka on ice.

Rupert

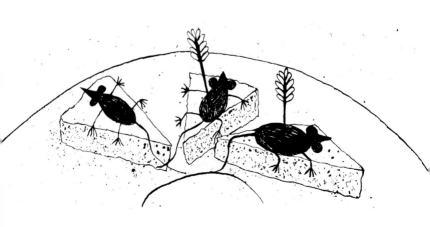

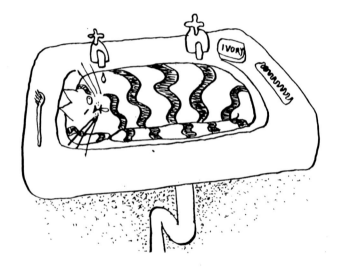

Sophie

Sophie the cat
sought the sink for her naps
and delighted in tonguing
the drips from the taps.

…

Theodore

Theodore the cat
trapped himself in a towel,
then stood up and walked
like a monk in a cowl.

Ursula

Ursula the cat
—under-the-weather all season—
had no desire to be social,
whatever the reason.

Vaughn the cat
vamped at the neighborhood pub
doing three shows a night
for a beer and some grub.

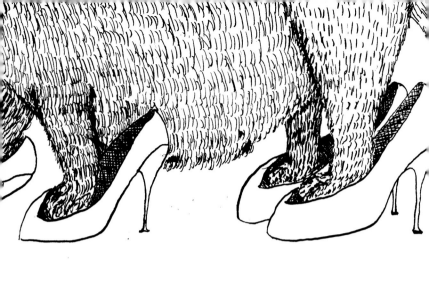

Whitney the cat
walked to manage her weight
in a smart set of shoes
in a generous size eight.

Xavier the cat
X'd his name in cement
and then proudly sat down
with no need to repent.

Xavier

WET
CEMENT

Safe

direction
indicator
or alert

Playful

danger danger?!

tails

Yolanda the cat
yammered all day on the phone
and though no one had called,
she was never alone.

Yolanda

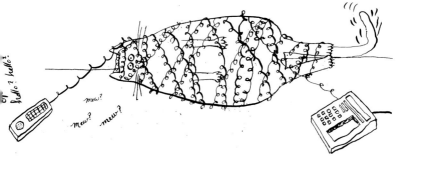

hello? hello?

mew?

mew? mew?

Zack

Zack the cat,
zealous in claiming his space,
defined his spot clearly
beneath the staircase.

If Alex Boies, *artist, isn't laboring under the influence of pen and ink, it must be summertime, when she's up to her elbows in loam and peat, devising delightful gardens and creating summertime havens for her Minnesota friends . . . often attended by Belle, Alex's Bouvier de Flanders beauty, dwarfing her mistress and defying the sultry sun in her thick, iridescent, blue-black coat.*

Jo Davison, *graphic designer, infuses her days with color, typography, imagery, and art, creating magical connections between brands and audiences . . . and when she can steal the time, she's tending her flowers and herbs with LuLu (a rescued parakeet who swings and sings in her delicate cage) and Murray (her splendid English springer spaniel who stains his liver-and-white coat green as he rolls in the thick grass, rejoicing at her side).*

A wolf by any other name, Horace P. Bogartus II— lovingly known by Tim Hodapp, *writer, as Bogart— is the black standard poodle who, snout on paws, peers up through long lashes, cobalt eyes focused, tail still . . . patiently waiting for Tim to finally lift his head from the papers, pens, and books on his writing desk and speak words of true meaning: "Treat?" "Walk?" "Park?" As the tail goes, so go they.*

Purr Purr Purr

Purr Purr Purr

Purr Purr Purr

Purr Purr P

Purr

Scratch Sc

Purr Purr P

Purr Purr P

Purr Purr

Purr Purr P

Purr Purr

Purr Purr

Purr

Purr Purr

lick lick lick

ty lickety lick

lick lick lick

lick lick li

cough cough c

h ← furball la

lick lick li

ty lick lick l

ick lick lick lick